Golden Legacy of Spain

Shaykh Mufti Saiful islām Sāhib

JKN Publications

First Published in April 2017

ISBN: 978-1-909114-15-9

British Library Cataloguing in Publication Data
A catalogue record for this book is available from the British Library.

Publisher's Note:

Every care and attention has been put into the production of this book. If how-ever you find any errors, they are our own, for which we seek Allāh's ﷻ for-giveness and reader's pardon.

Published by:

JKN Publications
118 Manningham Lane
Bradford
West Yorkshire
BD8 7JF
United Kingdom

t: +44 (0) 1274 308 456 | w: www.jkn.org.uk | e: info@jkn.org.uk

Book Title: Golden Legacy of Spain

Author: Shaykh Mufti Saiful Islām

Printed by Mega Printing in Turkey

"In the Name of Allāh, the Most Beneficent,
the Most Merciful"

Contents

Foreword

All praises are due to Allāh ﷻ —the Magnificent Lord of all creation. May endless peace and blessings be upon our beloved leader and guide, Muhammad ﷺ , his family, his Companions and those that follow their ways until the Day of Judgement.

Alhamdulillāh, Islām is a beautiful way of life that has reached every part of the globe. When we read about the lives of our pious predecessors, we see that they gave up their lives to spread the ultimate message of the oneness of Allāh ﷻ and the teachings of the Final Prophet Muhammad ﷺ. It is only when we truly research and study their lives, are we able to appreciate the sacrifices they made for the Deen.

With Andalus having a very rich legacy of Islām, our beloved Shaykh, Mufti Saiful Islām Sāhib travelled to recollect this memorable heritage and furthermore, to educate us about Spain's Golden Legacy during the Muslim rule. Inspite of Mufti Sāhib's busy schedule, other commitments and invitation to other countries, he prioritises his visits to those countries that contain rich Islamic heritage.

Upon his return, Mufti Sāhib shared some of his experiences with his students, reminiscing the glorious age of the Muslims. He explained to us the magnificent architectural constructions of the Masājd, the beautiful fountains and so on. All of these are the remanences of the Muslims which stand until this very day. As a student of Mufti Sāhib, this inspired me and kindled a desire in my heart to one day visit Andalus Inshā-Allāh to witness these remanences for myself.

This book explains the long-lost history of Islamic Spain and presents fascinating pictures,. It is hoped that this book will benefit the readers and provide an insight to the Spain's rich Islamic heritage.

It was a great privilege for me to transcribe Mufti Sāhib's notes into a book format and I pray that Allāh ﷻ rewards our beloved Shaykh for sharing such fruitful information and knowledge with us, elevate his ranks and allow the reader to fully reap the benefits of this book, Āmīn. I pray that Allāh ﷻ gives each and every one of us a chance to visit these sights. May Allāh ﷻ elevate the ranks of our Shaykh, his colleagues and his loved ones and those that helped with the compilation of this book.

Yumna Ahmad (Doncaster)
Student of JKN Institute (March 2017)

بِسْمِ اللهِ الرَّحْمٰنِ الرَّحِيْمِ

Introduction

In my student days, I was always fascinated by the history of Spain. After graduating, I studied the magnificent and tremendous rich history of this once, historical great Islamic country. It so happened, that many of my colleagues visited the country and narrated to me the beautiful Islamic legacy that once reigned in the heart of Europe.

Alhamdulillāh, Allāh ﷻ accepted my Du'ās and my close friend and colleague, brother Dilwār, the assistant Head Teacher of Green Lane Primary School, booked our tickets alongside another three colleagues, my close friend Maulāna Zubair Sūfi Sāhib, my dear colleague and student Maulāna Ātif Anwar Sāhib, and my companion in Hajj and Umrah , Maulāna Abdus-Salām Sāhib.

We travelled to this auspicious place on Monday 24th October 2016 for a few days. In this short treatise, I have combined both my knowledge and experience of Andalus with the sole purpose of educating the Muslims of this great legacy. I sincerely hope the readers will benefit immensely from this and pray that Allāh ﷻ accept this humble effort of mine, Āmīn.

(Shaykh Mufti) Saiful Islām Sāhib
Principal of JKN Institute
March 2017/Rajab 1438

Legacy of the Four Imāms

Prior to my journey, there were few programs I had to first priori-
tise and ensure they were completed successfully.

Firstly, the fundraising event on Friday 21st October 2016 before
Jumu'ah, was organised to raise donations for the reconstruction of
Tawakkulia Jāmi Masjid. I briefly addressed the gathering explain-
ing about the virtues and importance of spending in the path of
Allāh ﷻ, and the need for a Maktab and Masjid. Alhamdulillāh,
within ten to fifteen minutes, about £150,000 was pledged from the
generous congregation. Alhamdulillah, this program became suc-
cessful.

Secondly, conducting our weekly Tafsīr which regularly took place
on Saturday after Isha Salāh. Alhamdulillāh, by the grace of Allāh
ﷻ, I managed to complete the Tafsīr of three Juzz of the Holy
Qur'ān in three years and on Saturday I was commencing the
fourth Juzz from the back - Sūrah Dhāriyāt. The commentary of the
first Rukū was delivered on the topic of Jannah and Jahannam and
their inmates. After the Tafsīr session, I briefly met my mother and
bid her farewell.

Thirdly, JKN hosted a conference to discuss the legacy of the four
Imāms. A few months before, this programme was discussed by
many senior Ulamā in the monthly meeting that takes place on the
last Saturday of every month. All the scholars unanimously agreed
on the importance of this topic and it was decided that the programme is scheduled for Saturday 22nd October 2016. I, along with

Maulāna Ikhlāsur-Rahmān Sāhib finalised the speakers and Maulāna Urfān Sāhib made the posters and flyers.

For the conference, the following scholars were invited giving them specific topics to speak on. The programme was chaired by this humble servant and co-ordinated by Maulāna Ikhlāsur-Rahmān Sāhib and Maulāna Saiful Ālam Sāhib. Our chief guest was our beloved teacher, Shaykhul-Hadīth Maulāna Bilāl Sāhib – the last Khalīfah of Shaykhul-Hadīth, Maulāna Muhammad Zakariya ۩ who spoke towards the end in Urdu on 'The Legacy of the Four Imāms, which refreshed and boosted everyone's Imān and spirituality. His influential and mesmerising speech left everyone in tears and deep thoughts. Coupled with this, he frequently told jokes to waken up the spirit of the audience.

Mufti Abdul Muntaqim Sāhib from London spoke on 'The Language of the Friday Khutbah' in Urdu which was very elaborative and informative, Māshā-Allāh. Mufti Sāhib is a great Scholar with a bright future ahead, Inshā-Allāh.

Mufti Sirāj Sāleh Sāhib, one of our senior Hadīth teachers spoke on Imām Abū Hanīfah ۩ in Urdu in a very passionate way. Alhamdulillāh, the speech proved very beneficial for the audience which at that time was brimming to its peak in numbers. The entire hall was packed with scholars, elders, youngsters and students from all around the UK.

Shaykh Faizul Haq Abdul Azīz Sāhib from Birmingham spoke in English about 'The Status of the Four Imāms' in a very eloquent and articulate way. He fully captivated the audience in a loud and passionate voice.

Shaykh Emdādur-Rahmān Madni Sāhib spoke on a pertinent topic – 'Tarāwīh: Eight or Twenty?' A topic which has become very controversial nowadays. It is worth noting that the scholars have unanimously practiced reading twenty rak'ats for the past 1400 years. It was only until recently a fringe of scholars departed from the mainstream practice advocating eight rak'ats to be performed. The respected Shaykh spoke in Bangla quoting Arabic text and strong evidences proving that Tarāwīh is twenty rak'ats and not eight.

Dr Maulāna Rafāqat Rashid Sāhib - a senior teacher at JKN Institute, spoke on the unity of the Muslim Ummah within the four Imāms without causing any division and rivalry amongst us. Mufti Abdul Waheed Sāhib - the assistant Mufti of JKN Institute and a teacher of Fiqh touched on Imām Abū Hanīfah's ﷺ vast knowledge of Hadīth.

It is quite ironic for many of our youngsters to look down upon the great Imām Abū Hanīfah ﷺ and slander him of being weak in his knowledge of Hadīth without proper verification of the facts. Alhamdulillāh, through these speeches this misconception was erased. Maulāna Muhammad Yāsir Hanafi Sāhib addressed the gathering with a crucially important topic, 'Should I follow a Madhab?' He proved beyond any shadow of doubt, the importance of Taqlīd and the dangerous consequences of leaving Taqlīd.

Alhamdulillāh, the conference was a great success and it boosted everyone's Imān and knowledge. I was inundated with messages and emails alongside verbal compliments about the benefits of the programme. In fact, it was so productive that immediately part two was announced by our respected teacher Shaykhul-Hadīth Maulāna Bilāl Sāhib and I booked him and other scholars in the following year ,22nd of October 2017.

The conference commenced at 3pm and lasted till 10pm. It was a unique, refreshing programme and everyone who attended thoroughly enjoyed it, coupled with the thousands who were able to watch live on YouTube and listen to the online stream via Mixlr. May Allāh ﷻ accept our efforts and make it a means of our salvation in the hereafter, Āmīn.

Preparation for the Journey

After the programme 'The Legacy of the Four Imāms,' I had to meet up with the hundreds of brothers and well-wishers who wanted to express their appreciation and gratitude for holding this very beneficial and inspiring programme. Many Ulamā Kirām came from far and wide to attend this gathering and they remained with me till twelve o'clock midnight.

My close friend, Maulāna Zubair Sūfi Sāhib remained in my house till 3 am resting, whilst I made the last minute preparations. Brother Mustafa, the van driver arrived to my residence at 3am, followed by my other three colleagues who intended to travel with me. I bid my family farewell and headed towards Manchester Airport. We went through the baggage customs, performed Wudhu and boarded the plane, Easy Jet flight. We performed our Fajr Salāh on the plane in its beginning time which coincided with the flight time at 6.15am. After the flight lasting two hours and fifty minutes, we landed at Malaga Airport in Spain. We came out and met our van driver who was waiting outside with a placard having our brother Dilwār Hussain's name on it. After a two hour journey to Granada, we reached to our hotel.

Our hotel's name was Orol Del – Derro Suites 51, Albayzin Granada. This hotel is set in a historical 18th century building. The hotel was only 400 metres from the centre of Granada and from our balcony, we could easily view the magnificent and historical Alhambra.

An image of the hotel in which we stayed

After performing our Zuhr Salāh and a lunch which was kindly brought by our colleague Maulāna Ātif from home, we took a nap due to extreme tiredness of the journey. After performing our Asr Salāh in the hotel, we set off for Masjid-Taqwa which was in the vicinity of Alhambra. Alhamdulillāh, we managed to get there in time for the congregation of Maghrib Salāh in the Masjid.

An inside view of Masjid-Taqwa

Whilst walking to the Masjid, it reminded me and my colleagues who have all travelled to Masjid Al Aqsa as well, of the cobble roads and streets of Al-Quds. The roads and buildings were very historical and ancient in every aspect.

13

Awjazul-Masālik

After Maghrib Salāh, I remained seated with my colleagues and browsed through some of the Arabic books in the Masjid library. All the books relating to Māliki Fiqh, Hadīth and Tafsīr were found there which prompted me to think that the Masjid worshippers are adhering to the Māliki Fiqh.

I was extremely happy to see a set of Awjazul Masālik within the collection of books. Awjazul Masālik is the commentary of Muwatta Imām Mālik ﷺ in 15 volumes. Awjaz is a unique work of our great scholar and spiritual mentor, Shaykhul Hadīth Maulāna Muhammad Zakariya ﷺ. It explains the Māliki School in detail and also other schools of thought. It also includes spiritual explanation of Ahādīth and Shaykh's own masterly and unique interpretation of Hadīth.

Long live our great scholars and predecessors! How ecstatic and jubilant I became to know about the Fuyūz (blessings) of our elders spread throughout the worlds, even after the decline of Islām in Spain.

I browsed through other commentaries in these few minutes, including a Tafsīr attributed to the great Companion, Sayyidunā Abdullāh Ibn Mas'ūd ﷺ named as Tafsīr Ibn Mas'ūd. The compiler Māshā-Allāh did an excellent job of gathering the quotes and Tafsīr from a number of Tafāsīr (commentaries). All in all, he referenced every Tafsīr from all the major Hadīth books and Tafsīr books. From the Ahādīth collection, for example –

- Muwatta Mālik,
- Musnad Rabī Ibn Habīb,
- Musnad Imām Shāfi'ī,
- Musnad Imām Ahmad,
- Bukhāri,
- Muslim,
- Abū Dāwūd,
- Nasai,
- Tirmizī
- Ibn Mājah.

From the Tafsīr collection, he referenced it with the following –

- Tafsīr-Tabarī,
- Tārīkh-Tabarī,
- Al-Masāhif-Li-Ibn-Abī-Dāwūd,
- Al-Mustadrak-Lil-Hākim,
- Asbāb-Un-Nuzūlul-Qur'ān-Wāhidi,
- Tafsīrul-Baghawī (Ma'ālimut-Tanzīl),
- Tafsīruz-Zamakhsharī (Al Kashshāf),
- Tafsīr Ibnul Jawzī 🏵 (Zādul-Masīr),
- Tafsīr Rāzi (Mafātīhul Ghāib),
- Tafsīr Qurtubi (Al Jāmi-Li-Ahkāmil Qur'ān),
- Tafsīr Baydhāwi (Anwarut Tanzīl),
- Takhlīsul Mustadrak Liz-Zahabi 🏵,
- Tafsīrul Qur'ānil Azīm (Tafsīr Ibn-Kathīr 🏵),
- Al-Kāfi-Ash-Shāfi-Ibn-Hajr 🏵,
- Tafsīr Suyūti (Ad-Durrul Manthūr)

Imām Qurtubi 🕮

I was fascinated by all the different works of Imām Qurtubi 🕮 which were available in this small library. From my student days, I studied Tafsīr Qurtubi and also about the rich legacy he left behind in Spain, as well as his contribution in the field of Tafsīr, Fiqh and Hadīth.

Imām Abū Abdillāh Al-Qurtubi Al-Ansāri 🕮 was a famous Muhaddith and Faqīh (jurist) from Cordoba of Māliki Fiqh. He is most famous for his commentary of the Qur'ān, Tafsīr Qurtubi. Imām Qurtubi 🕮 was born in 1214 AD in Cordoba, Spain. His father was a farmer and died during a Spanish attack in 1230 AD. He received his elementary education in Cordoba. After the fall of Cordoba, he left for Alexandria, where he studied Hadīth, Tafsīr and Fiqh. In his later life he moved to Cairo and settled at a place in Munya. He died in Egypt on 29th April 1273 at the age of 59.

He has written several books,
1.   Tafsīr Qurtubi – this is a 20 volume commentary and has many editions. It is not only limited to Tafsīr as its name implies but is a general interpretation of the whole of the Qur'ān with a Māliki point of view. Every verse has been explained in thorough detail with all relevant evidences and proofs from authentic sources.
2. Ath-Tadhkirah-Fī-Ahwā-Lil-Mawtā-Wa-Umūril-Ākhirah
(Reminder of the Conditions of the Dead and the Matters of the Hereafter) – a book dealing with the subject of death, the punish-

ment of the grave, the end of time and the Day of Judgement.

3. Al-Asnā-Fī-Sharhil-Asmāil Husnā

4. Kitābut-Tadhkār-Fī-Afdhalil-Adhkār

5. At-Taqrīb Li Kitābit-Tahmīd

6. Kitāb-Kāmilul-Hirs Biz-Zuhdi Wal-Qanā'ati

Other Islamic Scholars of Andalusia

1. Abū-Ishāq Ash-Shātibi ﷺ (1320 AD — 1388 AD)

Ibrāhīm Ibn Mūsa Ibn Muhammad Ash Shātibi Al Gharnāti ﷺ descended from the tribe of Banū Lakhm. Imām Shātibi ﷺ was a follower of the Māliki Fiqh who passed away in Granada. He was a Faqīh (jurist) and had written many books amongst which the best known are Al Muwāfaqāt fi Usūlish-Sharī'ah (4 volumes) and Al-I'tisām (related to defining innovations).

2. Abū Muhammad Yahyā Al-Laythi ﷺ (Died 848 AD)

Yahyā Al-Laythi ﷺ was the pioneer for introducing the Māliki Fiqh in Andalus. His grandfather participated in the Muslim conquest of Iberia by Tāriq Ibn-Ziyād. Later, his grandfather was appointed as a governor of certain territories by the first leader of Cordoba - Abdur-Rahmān. Yahyā Al-Laythi ﷺ travelled to the east at a young age and studied under Imām Mālik ﷺ and was later re-

garded as the most important transmitter of Imām Mālik ﷺ's Muwatta. Returning to Andalus, he focused on his teacher's scholarly
work. As a member of the Shūra (the advisory board for the Amīrs
and judges) – he had an enormous influence on the nomination of
legal positions. Still, he himself never accepted a legal position. In
his role as a member of the Shūra, he became close to the ruler of
Andalus, who was apparently impressed with his intelligence and
authority on Islamic matters. He thus grew to become the most influential member of the Shūra, giving him the opportunity to nom-
inate judges, who also favoured the Māliki school. Towards the
end of his life, the Māliki school dominated Andalus through his
efforts.

3. Qādhi Iyādh Ibn-Mūsa ﷺ (1083 AD—1149 AD)

Qādhi Iyādh Ibn-Mūsa ﷺ was born into an established family of
Arab origin in Ceuta. In belonging to a notable scholarly family,
Qādhi Iyādh ﷺ was able to learn from the best teacher Ceuta had
to offer. The judge Abū Abdillāh Muhammad Ibn Mūsa ﷺ was
Qādhi Iyādh's ﷺ first important teacher. Though Qādhi Iyādh ﷺ
wasn't born in Andalus, he benefitted from the scholars of Andalus. He became a prestigious scholar in his own right and won the
support of the highest levels of society. In his quest for knowledge,
Qādhi Iyādh ﷺ spent some time visiting Cordoba, Murcia, Almeria
and Granada. He received Ijāzah (permission) from the most important scholars of his time, Abū Ali As-Sadafi ﷺ in Murcia, and
met with some of the most renowned scholars such as Ibnul-Hajj ﷺ
and Ibn-Rushd ﷺ. Qādhi Iyādh ﷺ was a Faqīh and was also appointed the judge of Granada.

4. Ibn-Rushd ﷺ (1126 AD — 1198 AD)

Ibn-Rushd ﷺ (Averroes) was born in Cordoba to a family with a long and well respected tradition of legal and public services. His grandfather Abul-Walīd Muhammad was a chief judge of Cordoba, under the Almoravids. His father Abul-Qāsim Ahmad held the same position until the Almoravids were replaced by the Almohads in 1146. Ibn-Rushd's ﷺ education followed a traditional path, beginning with studies in Hadīth, linguistics, jurisprudence and scholastic theology. He wrote on many subjects including logic, philosophy, theology, Māliki Fiqh, psychology, politics, geography, mathematics, medicine, astronomy, physics and celestial mechanics. Ibn-Rushd ﷺ died in Marrakesh, which is present day Morocco. The 13th century philosophical movement in Latin Christian and Jewish tradition based on Ibn-Rushd's works is called Averroism.

The Masjid plaque named after Ibn Rushd ﷺ

5. Ibn-Zuhr ﷺ (1094 AD — 1162 AD)

Ibn Zuhr ﷺ (Avenzoar) was a physician, surgeon and a poet. He was born at Seville in Andalusia and was the well-regarded physician of his era. He was particularly known for his emphasis on a more rational emphatic basis of medicine. His major works, Ath-Taysīr fil-Mudāwāt wath-Tadbīr, (Book of Simplification concerning Therapeutics and Diets.) was translated into Latin and Hebrew and was influential for the progress of surgery. He also improved surgical and medical knowledge by identifying several disease and treatments. Ibn-Zuhr ﷺ performed the first experimental tracheotomy on a goat.

6. Abul-Qāsim Az-Zahrāwi ﷺ (936 AD — 1013 AD)

Abul-Qāsim Az-Zahrāwi ﷺ was born in the city of Az-Zahra, 8km North West of Cordoba. Abul-Qāsim is considered as one of the greatest surgeons in history and has been named as the father of surgery. His greatest contribution to medicine is his book, Kitābut-Tasrīf, a 30 volume encyclopaedia of medical practices. His pioneering contributions to the field of surgical procedures and instruments had an enormous influence in the east and west, well into the modern period, to the extent that some of his discoveries are still applied in medicine to this day. He was the first physician to describe an ectopic pregnancy, and the first physician to identify the hereditary nature of haemophilia. He lived most of his life in Cordoba, where he studied, taught and practiced medicine and surgery until shortly before his death in 1013 AD.

7. Ibn-Tufayl ﷺ (1105 AD - 1185 AD)

Ibn-Tufayl ﷺ born in Gaudix near Granada was a polymath credited also as a writer, novelist, philosopher, theologian, physician, astronomer and court official. As a philosopher and novelist, he is most famous for writing the first philosophical novel – Hayy Ibn-Yaqdhān, also known as Philosophus Autodidactus in the western world. As a physician, he was an early supporter of dissection and autopsy, which was expressed in his novel. He served as a secretary for the ruler of Granada and later as a minister and physician for Abū Yāqub Yūsuf, the Almohad Caliph, to whom he recommended Ibn Rushd as his own future successor in 1169.

8. Ibrāhīm Ibn Yahya Az-Zarkhali ﷺ (1029 AD-1087 AD)

Ibrāhīm Ibn Yahya Az-Zarkhali ﷺ was an Arab instrument maker, astrologer, and one of the leading astronomers of his time. His works inspired a generation of Islamic astronomers in Andalus. He was trained as a metal-smith and due to his skills he was nicknamed An-Naqqāsh, the engraver of metals. He was particularly talented in geometry and astronomy and his extensive experience and knowledge eventually made him the foremost astronomer of his time.

Masjid-Taqwa

I was also pleased to see the different programmes taking place in Masjid Taqwa of different Islamic sciences. There were sessions of Aqīdah, Sīrah and Fiqh taking place throughout the week. Before returning to our hotel, we browsed around the outside area of Alhambra and had a quick snack in one of the Arabian restaurants. After performing our Isha Salāh, we retired to bed.

Second Day of Our Journey

After performing our Fajr Salāh at 7am, two of our colleagues, Maulāna Ātif and brother Dilwār headed for the purchase of tickets for Alhambra. May Allāh ﷻ bless them, they had to queue up one and a half hours to purchase the tickets – so much demand and interest for this visit of Alhambra. After having a nice breakfast prepared by our Maulāna Ātif we caught a taxi to the entrance of Alhambra. It is only when we entered that we realised the true extent of the rich legacy of Islām in this particular location of the world.

Spanish Islām and Tāriq Ibn-Ziyād ۩

Islām dominated Andalusia (modern day Spain) and Portugal for over eight centuries, since the beginning of Umayyad conquest around 711 AD.

It all began when Tāriq Ibn-Ziyād ۩ led the Muslim army and crossed Gibraltar from the North African coast consolidating and strengthening his troops in Gibraltar, which was then called Jabal-e -Tāriq meaning 'Mountain of Tāriq'- named after him. Tāriq Ibn Ziyād's ۩ army consisted of 7,000 horsemen, who defeated the army of Roderic – The King of Spain. In history books, it mentions that he assembled 100,000 men against Tāriq Ibn-Ziyād ۩ but was utterly defeated and killed on July 19th at the Battle of Guadalete.

Sermon of Tāriq Ibn-Ziyād ۩

Many historians have mentioned a historical speech which Tāriq Ibn-Ziyād ۩ gave to his army prior to that particular battle. I would like to briefly mention some extracts from it.

"O' my army! Where will you flee? Behind you is the sea and in front of you is the enemy. You have only hope of your courage now and your steadfastness. Remember! In this country you are more unfortunate than the orphan seated at the table of his greedy master. Your enemy is in front of you, protected by a huge army. He has men in abundance, but you have only your sword as your aid. Your only chance of life is that what you can snatch from the hands of your enemies. If you delay to seize immediate success, your good success will vanish and your enemies whom your very

presence has filled with fear will take courage. Put your disgrace and hu-miliation to one side and attack the enemy who has left his strong fortified city to confront you. It is a golden opportunity to defeat them if you hap-pily put yourself forward for death. Do not think that I will endanger you all and withdraw myself from it. In the fierce attack, I will be at the fore-front where the chance of life is very bleak. Remember! O' my army, if you suffer few moments in patience, you will soon after enjoy supreme delight. Do not think your fate and destiny is different from mine. Be as-sured that if you fall, I shall perish with you or I will avenge you. The Commander of the Believers, Walīd-Ibn-Abdul-Malik has chosen you for this battle from all his Muslim warriors and he promises that you shall become his comrades and shall hold senior ranks in this country. Such is the confidence in your bravery and courage. The fruit which he desires to achieve from your bravery is that the word of Allāh should be exalted and elevated in this new country and that the true genuine religion shall be established here. The spoils of war shall belong to yourselves. I take charge of this army and Inshā-Allāh you will see me seeking out this king Roderic – the tyrant of his people, challenging him to a combat. If I perish after this, I will have had at least the satisfaction of leading you and you will find a role model hero amongst you. But should I fall before I reach to the tyrant Roderick, multiply your bravery and courage, force yourself to the attack and gain the conquest of this country by depriving him of life. With him dead, his army will no longer challenge you."

Tāriq Ibn Ziyād ﷺ in the Battlefield of Andalus

Below is an English translation of one of Allāmah Iqbāl's ﷺ famous poems about Tāriq Ibn-Ziyād's ﷺ courage and conquest. He titles it "Tāriq Undulus Ke Maydān May" (Tāriq in the city of Al-Andalus).

These victorious warriors, these amazing servants of Yours,
To whom You have bestowed the divine taste,
Who cleave the desert and river in twain,
Their terror transforms the mountains into dust.
They care not for the world, and they care not for its pleasures.
In their passion, in their zeal, in their love for You O' Lord,
Martyrdom is their objective, not the spoils of war, nor the fame or glory of the world.
You've united the warring dessert tribes,
in thoughts, in deeds and in the prayers.
The burning fire that life had sought for centuries was found in them at last.
They think of death not as life's end, but as the enhancer of the heart.
Revive in the hearts of the Muslim again, the slogan of 'Lā-Tazar' (O' Allāh! do not leave even one of the disbeliever) – the prayer of Nūh ﷺ '.
Awaken in them the strong iron will and make their eyes a sharpened sword.

Islamic Spain – A Brief Introduction

1. In 711 AD – Tāriq Ibn-Ziyād ☙ with the Muslim army invaded Spain and in seven years conquered the peninsula. By 720 AD, all of Spain fell under Muslim rule.

2. The Golden Age – 756 AD-1031 AD – This era started with Abdur-Rahmān I, who founded the emirates of Cordoba and managed to unite all the Muslims in Spain. This period saw the progress of education and learning where libraries, colleges, public baths were established and literature, poetry and architecture flourished. Both Muslims and non-Muslims made major contributions to this magnificent culture.

The Islamic civilisation reached it's peak in the 10th century and by 1100 AD, the number of Muslims rose to nearly 6 million. Andalus produced many great intellectuals, such as Ibn-Rushd ☙, Ibn-Zuhr ☙ (Avenzoar), Al-Khwārizmī ☙ (Algoritmi) and the likes of many more. It is from these great scholars that other faiths and religions took their philosophies and sciences.

3. The first Tāifas (1031-1091) – Andalus divided into small kingdom and ruled by a family or dynasty.

4. After the Golden Era came the Almoravid Era (1031-1130).

5. The Al-Mohad ruled from 1131-1238 AD

6. The Nasrids of The Kingdom of Granada (1238-1492 AD).

The Granada War began in 1482 against the Emirate of Granada. It took 10 years for the Catholic Monarchs, Isabella of Castile and Ferdinand of Aragon (on 2nd January 1492) to take the last remaining Muslim territory.

Inside Alhambra

Alhambra covers approximately 104,000 m². The city of Alhambra was protected by 30 towers and the ramparts which were around the perimeters.

There are three entrances to Alhambra - The Gate of Justice, The Gate of Weapons and The Gate of Seven Floors. There was a Madraza (university) located in the space between the Alcazaba (fortress) and the Machuca tower.

Myself and my colleagues paid 14 euros each for the entry fee into Alhambra and we utilised our few hours marvelling at the amazing and extraordinary structure of this miraculous monumental complex. I will only list the most important areas we visited in this short trip.

The map of Alhambra at the entrance

An image inside Alhambra

Obviously, you can write volumes and volumes regarding Alhambra and its historical significance.

1. Gate of Justice – built in 1348 by the Muslim ruler Yūsuf I.

2. The Alcazaba – This was the first of all the constructions in the Alhambra and the military area of the complex. Nearby, we visited the Round Tower, the Military Quarter, the Gate of Alms, the Watch Tower and Wall-Walk Garden.

An image of the Alcazaba

3. The Nasrid Palaces. There were three palaces built in three different periods:
   - Mexuar Palace – built during the reigns of Ismā'īl I (1314-1325 AD) and Muhammad V (1362-1391 AD)

- Comares Palace (Diwān) – built during the reigns of Yūsuf
I (1333-1354 AD) and Muhammad V (1362-1391 AD)
- Palace of the Lions (Harem) – built during the reign of
Muhammad V (1362-1391 AD)

An image near the Nasrid Palaces

4. The Partal and The Towers - This is where the most splendid towers were and its interior design resembled small palaces. This area included the portico of the palace, the gardens, the Rawdah, the Palace of Yūsuf III and other small towers.

5. Generalife – This was a recreational palace and estate, independent of the Alhambra, used by the Muslim leaders as a place of retreat and rest. It included the lower gardens, the palace of the Generalife and the upper gardens.

One of the most profound and outstanding feature of the Alhambra building is the calligraphy. Most of the content of the calligraphy decorating the walls of the building and ceilings are verses of the Holy Qur'ān. I was approached by many Muslims and non-Muslims during my tour to explain what was written in the calligraphy. The statement 'Lā Ghāliba illallāh – No one is dominant except Allāh ﷻ' is found over nearly every ceiling and wall of Alhambra. There is also poetry engraved on the walls and ceilings praising the palaces and its Muslim rulers. The two famous poets of the monuments are Ibn Zamrak and Ibn Yayyab.

An image showing the great detail of calligraphy inside Alhambra

During our visit, we performed our Wudhu with fresh clean water from the fountains of Alhambra and prayed our Zuhr Salāh in congregation whilst many of the visitors stared at us with surprise. Only Allāh ﷻ knows how I felt leading the Salāh in this historical place which once echoed with the greatness of Allāh ﷻ and the beautiful teachings of Islām in every corner.

An image of the fountains in Alhambra

We returned back to our hotel to perform our Asr and Maghrib Salāh. Thereafter we rested for a while to recuperate from the tiredness of the previous two nights. After performing Ishā Salāh in congregation, we had a light refreshment and I began studying the history of Alhambra until late night.

Third Day of Our Journey

We woke up early and performed our Fajr Salāh at the beginning time. After a quick breakfast, we headed for the coach station to visit Cordoba, a journey of three hours. We all purchased an open return ticket for 25 euros. The coach journey was very comfortable and we reached Cordoba around 11:30am. After purchasing a ticket for the entrance to Cordoba Mosque for 8 euros, we hastened to observe the long-lost legacy of our Islamic history.

Cordoba Mosque

The Grand Mosque of Cordoba is regarded as one of the most accomplished monuments of Islamic architecture. The sight was originally a small temple for the Catholic Christians. When the Muslims conquered Spain in 711 AD, the church was divided into Muslim and Christian halves. This sharing arrangement of the sight lasted until 784 AD. It was then that the Muslim leader Abdur-Rahmān I, purchased the Christian half and after demolishing the original structure, built the Grand Mosque of Cordoba on this ground. Cordoba returned to the Christians in 1236 AD and the building was converted to a Roman Catholic Church.

By looking at the decorations, the amount of material which were needed for this structure became clear. Ivory, gold, silver, copper, brass and many other metals were used in the decorations. Panels of scented woods were fastened with nails of pure gold and the red marble columns gave that beautiful look that Allāmah Iqbāl 🕮 describes its classical hall as having countless pillars like rows of

palm-trees. The Cordoba Masjid is most distinguished for its ar-
caded hall with 856 columns of marble and granite. The walls of
the Masjid had Quranic verses engraved on them which added to
the beauty. Alongside all this, the breath-taking tile work, calligraphy and architectural forms left me speechless.

Images inside the Cordoba Masjid

It was extremely saddening that we were clearly instructed not to perform our Salāh in the Cordoba Masjid compound but rather to pray in any other Masjid. These words grieved me immensely– that once an overcrowded Masjid which accommodated 15,000 people – now the condition is that we could not even individually pray two rak'ats of Salāh.

This reminded me of a lecture delivered by the renowned scholar, Shaykh Abul Hasan Ali Nadwi ﷺ when he visited the UK which I would like to present here for my readers to ponder and reflect upon.

Message for the Muslims in the West

Shaykh Sayyid Abul Hasan Ali Nadwi's ﷺ summary of a speech delivered in Urdu at Markaz, Dewsbury in 1982.

Your warm reception and friendliness is a source of great happiness for me. If I do not respect your wishes and express my inner feelings, I would be most ungrateful. If I desire, I could shower you with praises, for Almighty Allāh ﷻ has bestowed me with an abundance of vocabulary, but I would not be fulfilling the right of friendship.

As you are aware, the Prophet ﷺ had a burning desire to invite humanity to accept Islām. Despite 13 years of untiring effort in Makkah Mukarramah and 7 years in Madeenah Munawwarah, there was no large scale conversion of non-Muslims into Islām. However, between 7 AH and 10 AH, from after Fath-Makkah (the conquest of Makkah) until the Prophet's ﷺ demise, there was such an influx of people entering into Islām as was not witnessed in the preceding 20 years.

Imām Zuhri ﷺ, an eminent Muhaddith and Tābi'ee, expresses surprise on this sea of change, with so many people embracing Islām in a matter of just 3 years. He, along with other distinguished Muhaddithoon, have commented that this large scale conversion was due to non-Muslims having an opportunity, for the first time, to observe and intermingle with Muslims, witnessing their honesty, fair dealing, compassion and their sole reliance on Allāh ﷻ. This left such a deep and profound impression on non-Muslims that thousands entered into the fold of Islām within a relatively short period of time.

This incident also contains abundant lessons on how Muslims should live in this country. Their conduct should be so sublime and captivating that whosoever sees them, accepts Islām. Whosoever sits with us should be inclined towards Islām. There should be no need to convince anyone to accept the Truth.

Therefore, in this country, if you wish to live peacefully and have an opportunity to present Islām to the host community, you will need to inculcate and manifest brilliant qualities, not just inside the Masājid but also outside in the streets, in the markets, in your daily activities and at home. A life of Taqwa will immediately attract non-Muslims towards Islām.

As an ordinary student of Islām, it is my religious responsibility to warn you. If you do not lead an upright life, if you continue to live a narrow-minded lifestyle and if you fail to manifest the beauty of Islām to non-Muslims, then you will face real dangers. In such a case, there is no reason for you to feel content and secure in this country.

If ever the fire of race, religion or nationalism rages here, then you will not be saved. In Spain, there were Masājid a hundred times more beautiful than yours, so do not feel content and self-satisfied. As an ordinary student of religion, I would wish to express my joy and happiness at this wonderful new Masjid, but how shall I con-gratulate you on your achievement, when the words of congratula-tion are self-evident on the walls. How better can I compliment you?

Others may not speak to you as plainly, but remember the glorious Masjid-e-Cordova still stands in Spain. Iqbal so eloquently remi-nisces the great legacy of Islamic Spain in his famous poem 'Masjid -e-Qurtuba'. In Islamic Spain there were such brilliant Masājid, cel-ebrated Madāris and famous scholars, for instance Shaikh-e-Akbar, Ibn Hazm, Qurtubi, Shātbi - and how many others shall I mention? However, when the flames of religious sectarianism raged, then the Masājid and Madāris became deserted. Once, Islamic Spain boasted such magnificent structures, distinguished educational centres, and a refined culture and society. Regrettably, the Mus-lims, despite such a high standard of living, did not draw the na-tive non-Muslims of that country to see the truth of Islām and warn them of the dangers of disbelief, with the result that religions subsequently consumed Muslims like a morsel. The Arabs, with their glowing history, architectural splendour and vast ocean of knowledge, were displaced from the country and today, the ears eagerly wait to hear the Adhān and the empty Masājid thirst for your Salāh.

You must earn your place in this country. You should leave an im-print on the host community of your usefulness. You must demon-strate that your existence here is more beneficial than that of the native people. You must impart on them the lessons of humanity.

You should demonstrate how noble and principled you are, and that there cannot be found more upright humans elsewhere besides you. You need to establish your worth and that you are a blessing and mercy for this country. However, if you decide to live in an enclosed environment, content with your prayers and fasting, apathetic to the people and society you live in and never introducing them to the high Islamic values and your own personal qualities, then beware, lest any religion or sectarianism flares up. In such a situation you will not find safety.

I pray to Almighty Allāh ﷻ that my prediction is totally untrue and baseless. Remember, you are guests here. Your Tablīgh, Masājid, Madāris, Ibādah and religious sacrifices are all worthy of commendation. May Almighty Allāh ﷻ grant you Barakah, but do not forget to earn your place in this country. Gain mastery of the national language and become proficient so that you can use it effectively to propagate Islām. Prepare writers and orators and although you will distance yourself from their religion, do not distance yourself from them. Earn credibility through your daily activities, so much so that if you are entrusted with difficult responsibilities, as was Prophet Yūsuf ﷺ, you do not avoid but rather you embrace all challenges wholeheartedly.

You will have to present a new pattern of life to this country. You will not earn recognition by exerting yourselves in the workplace. If you overwork, you will be looked upon disparagingly and be likened to horses and bulls and labelled as money-making machines. However, if you can show to the natives here that you are worshippers of Allāh ﷻ and not wealth, that you do not bow before power but only before virtue, that you are humans and think like humans, that you are concerned not only about yourselves but also about others, that you are compassionate not just to your own children but also to theirs and to them, and that you are earnestly concerned about the path of destruction they have chosen for themselves then you will earn their respect. They will begin to respect Islām and become desirous of studying it. They will ask you for literature concerning Islamic beliefs and practices and an opportunity will arise here for you to propagate Islām.

However, if you remain preoccupied in eating and working and engaged in prayers, indifferent to what is happening in the country, insulated within Muslims and totally apathetic to what is happening outside and which direction the country is heading, in such a situation, if there is any trouble, you will not be able to save yourselves.

I have been meaning to convey and emphasise this message to you, because I do not know whether I will be able to visit you in the future. You gathered here with love and affection and therefore it was easy for me. As a student of religion, it would have been convenient for me to suggest virtues of reciting various Dhikr or prescribe certain Wazīfahs, but you might not have had an opportunity of listening to the message I have just conveyed from anyone else.

Please strengthen your position in this country and earn your recognition. Do not be like a straw or crop that is uprooted by the slightest breeze. You should be so firm that not even a hurricane is able to shift you. Display such noble character that you enslave the natives. Then see how these people will stand to defend you. If there is the slightest opposition against you, they will be the first ones to argue on your behalf and vouch what a blessing you are for them.

May Almighty Allāh 🌼 grant us the ability to understand what is right; may He bless and protect you. Āmīn.

Allāmah Iqbāl's 🌼 Poem Regarding Spain

Whilst mentioning the message of Shaykh Abul Hasan Ali Nadwi 🌼, I thought it was also relevant to mention Allāmah Iqbāl's 🌼 poem, which he wrote on his return from Spain.

Spain! You are the trustee of the Muslim blood,
In my eyes you are sacred like the Haram.
Signs of Sajdah (prostration) lie hidden in your dust,
Silent calls to prayer are evident in your morning breeze.
In your hills and valleys were the tents of those individuals,
Whose tips of their lances were bright like the stars.
Is more henna needed by your beloved?
My own blood can give them some colour.
How can a Muslim be put down by the straw and grass?
Even if its flame has lost its heat and fire!
My eyes watched Granada as well,
But the traveller is neither content in journey nor at home.

41

I observed as well as demonstrated, I spoke as well as listened,
Neither seeing nor hearing brings calm to the heart.

Our Return From Cordoba Masjid

After the visit, we performed our Zuhr Salāh in one of the local Masjids and then we ate a Falafil sandwich from the restaurant of the Imām which was adjacent to the Masjid. There we met other Muslim brothers and sisters and families who were all looking for a place to perform their Zuhr Salāh.

We returned back to Granada at 7.30pm and read our Maghrib Salāh in the central Masjid of Garnāta (Granada). This was our final night of our three day trip.

An image inside the Central Masjid of Granada

Before I conclude, I would like to mention the poem that Allāmah Iqbāl 🕮 mentioned when he was returning from Cordoba, which is very heart-rendering and emotional. I will just quote some couplets from it as a taster.

He commences by this couplet,

The succession of day and night is the architect of events,
The succession of day and night is the fountain head of life and death.

Further on he says,

Your foundations are lasting, your columns countless,
Like the profusion of palms in the plains of Syria.
Your arches, your terraces, shimmer with the light.
That once flashed in the valley of Ayman.
Your soaring minarets all glow in the resplendence of Jibrīl's glory.
Stars look up on your precinct as a piece of heaven
But for centuries, alas!
Your minarets have not resonated with the call of the Muaddhin.
Were I to lift the veil of the profile of my reflections,
The West would be dazzled by its brilliance.

Subhān-Allāh, how beautifully Allāmah Iqbāl 🕮 has drawn a picture of the once great Masjid of Cordoba. May Allāh 🕮 make it a means of steadfastness on our Dīn. May He make this an eye opener for myself and the Muslims to value our Dīn till our last moments, Āmīn!

Other titles from JKN Publications

Your Questions Answered

An outstanding book written by Shaykh Mufti Saiful Islām. A very comprehensive yet simple Fatāwa book and a source of guidance that reaches out to a wider audience i.e. the English speaking Muslims. The reader will benefit from the various answers to questions based on the Laws of Islām relating to the beliefs of Islām, knowledge, Sunnah, pillars of Islām, marriage, divorce and contemporary issues.

UK RRP: £7.50

Hadeeth for Beginners

A concise Hadeeth book with various Ahādeeth that relate to basic Ibādāh and moral etiquettes in Islām accessible to a wider readership. Each Hadeeth has been presented with the Arabic text, its translation and commentary to enlighten the reader, its meaning and application in day-to-day life.

UK RRP: £3.00

Du'ā for Beginners

This book contains basic Du'ās which every Muslim should recite on a daily basis. Highly recommended to young children and adults studying at Islamic schools and Madrasahs so that one may cherish the beautiful treasure of supplications of our beloved Prophet 🕌 in one's daily life, which will ultimately bring peace and happiness in both worlds, Inshā-Allāh.

UK RRP: £2.00

How well do you know Islām?

An exciting educational book which contains 300 multiple questions and answers to help you increase your knowledge on Islām! Ideal for the whole family, especially children and adult students to learn new knowledge in an enjoyable way and cherish the treasures of knowledge that you will acquire from this book. A very beneficial tool for educational syllabus.

UK RRP: £3.00

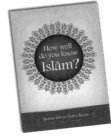

Treasures of the Holy Qur'ān

This book entitled "Treasures of the Holy Qur'ān" has been compiled to create a stronger bond between the Holy Qur'ān and the readers. It mentions the different virtues of Sūrahs and verses from the Holy Qur'ān with the hope that the readers will increase their zeal and enthusiasm to recite and inculcate the teachings of the Holy Qur'ān into their daily lives.

UK RRP: £3.00

Other titles from JKN PUBLICATIONS

Marriage - A Complete Solution

Islām regards marriage as a great act of worship. This book has been designed to provide the fundamental teachings and guidelines of all what relates to the marital life in a simplified English language. It encapsulates in a nutshell all the marriage laws mentioned in many of the main reference books in order to facilitate their understanding and implementation.

UK RRP: £5.00

Pearls of Luqmān

This book is a comprehensive commentary of Sūrah Luqmān, written beautifully by Shaykh Mufti Saiful Islām. It offers the reader with an enquiring mind, abundance of advice, guidance, counselling and wisdom.

The reader will be enlightened by many wonderful topics and anecdotes mentioned in this book, which will create a greater understanding of the Holy Qur'ān and its wisdom. The book highlights some of the wise sayings and words of advice Luqmān ﷺ gave to his son.

UK RRP: £3.00

Arabic Grammar for Beginners

This book is a study of Arabic Grammar based on the subject of Nahw (Syntax) in a simplified English format. If a student studies this book thoroughly, he/she will develop a very good foundation in this field, Inshā-Allāh. Many books have been written on this subject in various languages such as Arabic, Persian and Urdu. However, in this day and age there is a growing demand for this subject to be available in English .

UK RRP: £3.00

A Gift to My Youngsters

This treasure filled book, is a collection of Islamic stories, morals and anecdotes from the life of our beloved Prophet ﷺ, his Companions ﷺ and the pious predecessors. The stories and anecdotes are based on moral and ethical values, which the reader will enjoy sharing with their peers, friends, families and loved ones.

"A Gift to My Youngsters" – is a wonderful gift presented to the readers personally, by the author himself, especially with the youngsters in mind. He has carefully selected stories and anecdotes containing beautiful morals, lessons and valuable knowledge and wisdom.

UK RRP: £5.00

Travel Companion

The beauty of this book is that it enables a person on any journey, small or distant or simply at home, to utilise their spare time to read and benefit from an exciting and vast collection of important and interesting Islamic topics and lessons. Written in simple and easy to read text, this book will immensely benefit both the newly interested person in Islām and the inquiring mind of a student expanding upon their existing knowledge. Inspiring reminders from the Holy Qur'ān and the blessed words of our beloved Prophet ﷺ beautifies each topic and will illuminate the heart of the reader. **UK RRP: £5.00**

Pearls of Wisdom

Junaid Baghdādī ﷺ once said, "Allāh ﷻ strengthens through these Islamic stories the hearts of His friends, as proven from the Qur'anic verse,
"And all that We narrate unto you of the stories of the Messengers, so as to strengthen through it your heart." (11:120)
Mālik Ibn Dinār ﷺ stated that such stories are gifts from Paradise. He also emphasised to narrate these stories as much as possible as they are gems and it is possible that an individual might find a truly rare and invaluable gem among them. **UK RRP: £6.00**

Inspirations

This book contains a compilation of selected speeches delivered by Shaykh Mufti Saiful Islām on a variety of topics such as the Holy Qur'ān, Nikāh and eating Halāl. Having previously been compiled in separate booklets, it was decided that the transcripts be gathered together in one book for the benefit of the reader. In addition to this, we have included in this book, further speeches which have not yet been printed.

UK RRP: £6.00

Gift to my Sisters

A thought provoking compilation of very interesting articles including real life stories of pious predecessors, imaginative illustrations and much more. All designed to influence and motivate mothers, sisters, wives and daughters towards an ideal Islamic lifestyle. A lifestyle referred to by our Creator, Allāh ﷻ in the Holy Qur'ān as the means to salvation and ultimate success.

UK RRP: £6.00

Gift to my Brothers

A thought provoking compilation of very interesting articles including real life stories of pious predecessors, imaginative illustrations, medical advices on intoxicants and rehabilitation and much more. All designed to influence and motivate fathers, brothers, husbands and sons towards an ideal Islamic lifestyle. A lifestyle referred to by our Creator, Allāh ﷻ in the Holy Qur'ān as the means to salvation and ultimate success.

UK RRP: £5.00

Heroes of Islām
"In the narratives there is certainly a lesson for people of intelligence (understanding)." (12:111)

A fine blend of Islamic personalities who have been recognised for leaving a lasting mark in the hearts and minds of people.

A distinguishing feature of this book is that the author has selected not only some of the most world and historically famous renowned scholars but also these lesser known and a few who have simply left behind a valuable piece of advice to their nearest and dearest.   **UK RRP: £5.00**

Ask a Mufti (3 volumes)

Muslims in every generation have confronted different kinds of challenges. In-spite of that, Islām produced such luminary Ulamā who confronted and re-sponded to the challenges of their time to guide the Ummah to the straight path. "Ask A Mufti" is a comprehensive three volume fatwa book, based on the Hanafi School, covering a wide range of topics related to every aspect of human life such as belief, ritual worship, life after death and contemporary legal topics related to purity, commercial transaction, marriage, divorce, food, cosmetic, laws pertaining to women, Islamic medical ethics and much more.

UK RRP: £30.00

Should I Follow a Madhab?
Taqleed or following one of the four legal schools is not a new phenomenon. Historically, scholars of great calibre and luminaries, each one being a specialist in his own right, were known to have adhered to one of the four legal schools. It is only in the previous century that a minority group emerged advocating a se-vere ban on following one of the four major schools.

This book endeavours to address the topic of Taqleed and elucidates its im-portance and necessity in this day and age. It will also, by the Divine Will of Allāh ﷻ dispel some of the confusion surrounding this topic.   **UK RRP: £5.00**

Advice for the Students of Knowledge

Allāh ﷻ describes divine knowledge in the Holy Qur'ān as a 'Light'. Amongst the qualities of light are purity and guidance. The Holy Prophet ﷺ has clearly ex-plained this concept in many blessed Ahādeeth and has also taught us many supplications in which we ask for beneficial knowledge.

This book is a golden tool for every sincere student of knowledge wishing to mould his/her character and engrain those correct qualities in order to be wor-thy of receiving the great gift of Ilm from Allāh ﷻ.   **UK RRP: £3.00**

Stories for Children
"Stories for Children" - is a wonderful gift presented to the readers personally by the author himself, especially with the young children in mind. The stories are based on moral and ethical values, which the reader will enjoy sharing with their peers, friends, families and loved ones. The aim is to present to the children stories and incidents which contain moral lessons, in order to reform and correct their lives, according to the Holy Qur'ān and Sunnah.

UK RRP: £5.00

Pearls from My Shaykh

This book contains a collection of pearls and inspirational accounts of the Holy Prophet ﷺ, his noble Companions, pious predecessors and some personal accounts and sayings of our well-known contemporary scholar and spiritual guide, Shaykh Mufti Saiful Islām Sāhib. Each anecdote and narrative of the pious predecessors have been written in the way that was narrated by Mufti Saiful Islām Sāhib in his discourses, drawing the specific lessons he intended from telling the story. The accounts from the life of the Shaykh has been compiled by a particular student based on their own experience and personal observation. **UK RRP: £5.00**

Paradise & Hell

This book is a collection of detailed explanation of Paradise and Hell including the state and conditions of its inhabitants. All the details have been taken from various reliable sources. The purpose of its compilation is for the reader to contemplate and appreciate the innumerable favours, rewards, comfort and unlimited luxuries of Paradise and at the same time take heed from the punishment of Hell. Shaykh Mufti Saiful Islām Sāhib has presented this book in a unique format by including the Tafseer and virtues of Sūrah Ar-Rahmān. **UK RRP: £5.00**

Prayers for Forgiveness

Prayers for Forgiveness' is a short compilation of Du'ās in Arabic with English translation and transliteration. This book can be studied after 'Du'ā for Beginners' or as a separate book. It includes twenty more Du'ās which have not been mentioned in the previous Du'ā book. It also includes a section of Du'ās from the Holy Qur'ān and a section from the Ahādeeth. The book concludes with a section mentioning the Ninety-Nine Names of Allāh ﷻ with its translation and transliteration. **UK RRP: £3.00**

Scattered Pearls

This book is a collection of scattered pearls taken from books, magazines, emails and WhatsApp messages. These pearls will hopefully increase our knowledge, wisdom and make us realise the purpose of life. In this book, Mufti Sāhib has included messages sent to him from scholars, friends and colleagues which will be beneficial and interesting for our readers Inshā-Allāh. **UK RRP: £4.00**

Poems of Wisdom

This book is a collection of poems from those who contributed to the Al-Mumin Magazine in the poems section. The Hadeeth mentions "Indeed some form of poems are full of wisdom." The themes of each poem vary between wittiness, thought provocation, moral lessons, emotional to name but a few. The readers will benefit from this immensely and make them ponder over the outlook of life in general.

UK RRP: £4.00

This book is a detailed and informative commentary of the first three Sūrahs of the last Juz namely; Sūrah Naba, Sūrah Nāzi'āt and Sūrah Abasa. These Sūrahs vividly depict the horrific events and scenes of the Great Day in order to warn mankind the end of this world. These Sūrahs are an essential reminder for us all to instil the fear and concern of the Day of Judgement and to detach ourselves from the worldly pleasures. Reading this book allows us to attain the true realization of this world and provides essential advices of how to gain eternal salvation in the Hereafter.

RRP: £5:00

It is necessary that Muslims always strive to better themselves at all times and to free themselves from the destructive maladies. This book focusses on three main spiritual maladies; pride, anger and evil gazes. It explains its root causes and offers some spiritual cures. Many examples from the lives of the pious predecessors are used for inspiration and encouragement for controlling the above three maladies. It is hoped that the purification process of the heart becomes easy once the underlying roots of the above maladies are clearly understood.　　**UK RRP: £5:00**

This book is a step by step guide on Hajj and Umrah for absolute beginners. Many other additional important rulings (Masāil) have been included that will Insha-Allāh prove very useful for our readers. The book also includes some etiquettes of visiting (Ziyārat) of the Holy Prophet's 🕌 blessed Masjid and his Holy Grave.

UK　RRP　£3:00

This book contains essential guidelines for a spiritual Mureed to gain some familiarity of the science of Tasawwuf. It explains the meaning and aims of Tasawwuf, some understanding around the concept of the soul, and general guidelines for a spiritual Mureed. This is highly recommend-ed book and it is hoped that it gains wider readership among those Mureeds who are basically new to the science of Tasawwuf.

UK RRP £3:00

This book is a compilation of sayings and earnest pieces of advice that have been gathered directly from my respected teacher Shaykh Mufti Saiful Islām Sāhib. The book consists of many valuable enlightenments including how to deal with challenges of life, promoting unity, practicing good manners, being optimistic and many other valuable advices. Our respected Shaykh has gathered this Naseehah from meditating, contemplating, analysing and searching for the gems within Qur'anic verses, Ahādeeth and teachings of our Pious Predecessors. **UK RRP £1:00**

Kanzul Bāri

Kanzul Bāri provides a detailed commentary of the Ahādeeth contained in Saheeh al-Bukhāri. The commentary includes Imām Bukhāri's ﷺ biography, the status of his book, spiritual advice, inspirational accounts along with academic discussions related to Fiqh, its application and differences of opinion. Moreover, it answers objections arising in one's mind about certain Ahādeeth. Inquisitive students of Hadeeth will find this commentary a very useful reference book in the final year of their Ālim course for gaining a deeper understanding of the science of Hadeeth. **UK RRP: £15.00**

How to Become a Friend of Allāh ﷺ

The friends of Allāh ﷺ have been described in detail in the Holy Qur'ān and Āhadeeth. This book endeavours its readers to help create a bond with Allāh ﷺ in attaining His friendship as He is the sole Creator of all material and immaterial things. It is only through Allāh's ﷺ friendship, an individual will achieve happiness in this life and the Hereafter, hence eliminate worries, sadness, depression, anxiety and misery of this world. **UK RRP: £3.00**

Gems & Jewels

This book contains a selection of articles which have been gathered for the benefit of the readers covering a variety of topics on various aspects of daily life. It offers precious advice and anecdotes that contain moral lessons. The advice captivates its readers and will extend the narrowness of their thoughts to deep reflection, wisdom and appreciation of the purpose of our existence. **UK RRP: £4.00**

End of Time

This book is a comprehensive explanation of the three Sūrahs of Juzz Amma; Sūrah Takweer, Sūrah Infitār and Sūrah Mutaffifeen. This book is a continuation from the previous book of the same author, 'Horrors of Judgement Day'. The three Sūrahs vividly sketch out the scene of the Day of Judgement and describe the state of both the inmates of Jannah and Jahannam. Mufti Saiful Islām Sāhib provides an easy but comprehensive commentary of the three Sūrahs facilitating its understanding for the readers whilst capturing the horrific scene of the ending of the world and the conditions of mankind on that horrific Day. **UK RRP: £5.00**